BEING WITH YOU IS EVERYTHING

Discovering Your Baby's Voice

Dr. Heidelise Als devoted
her life's work to giving
premature and at-risk
infants a voice in shaping
their experiences
while in the hospital.

She founded NIDCAP*, an
individualized, nurturing
approach to care that
supports parents and families
in their most important role as
their baby's primary caregivers.

* NIDCAP stands for Newborn
Individualized Developmental
Care and Assessment Program

We are all connected;
we mutually support,
teach, learn from,
and enrich each other.

Heidelise Als, PhD

BEING WITH YOU IS EVERYTHING
Discovering Your Baby's Voice

Deborah Buehler, PhD

With drawings by
Annie Zeybekoglu

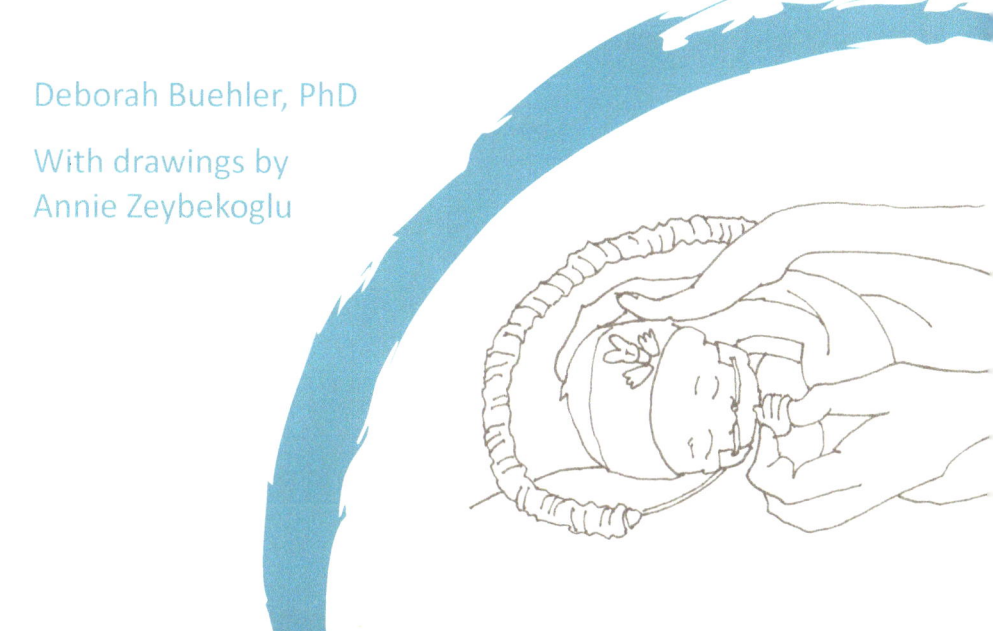

Endorsed by the NIDCAP Federation International, Inc.
The NIDCAP Federation International, Inc. logo is used with permission.

Printed and bound in the United States
ISBN: 978-1-966149-00-2

WHITE POPPY PRESS
An imprint of MODERN MEMOIRS, INC.

417 West Street, Suite 104
Amherst, Massachusetts 01002
413-253-2353
www.modernmemoirs.com

This book is dedicated to
your discovery of
your premature and/or
at-risk baby's voice and
the beauty of your unique,
evolving relationship.

In a strange place filled with humming and beeping, I stretch and squirm.

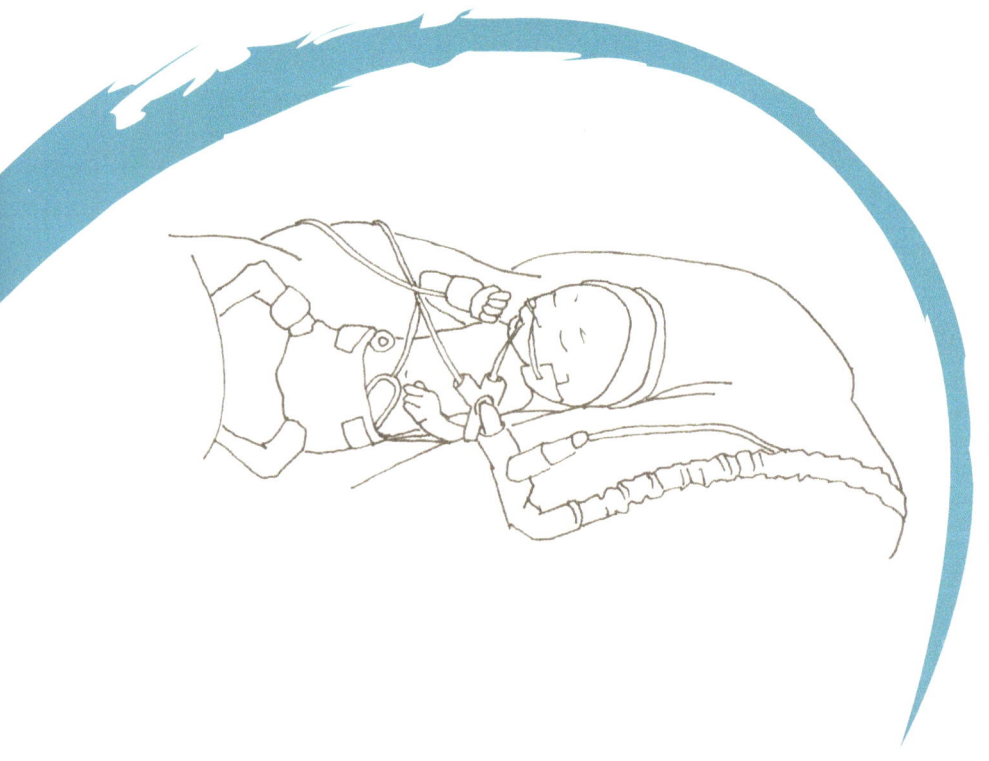

I am so small and delicate—yet I am here.

Relaxing sounds, soft light, and calm.
Every part of me feels soothed.

Whispering voices, a gentle touch,
I know that I am not alone.

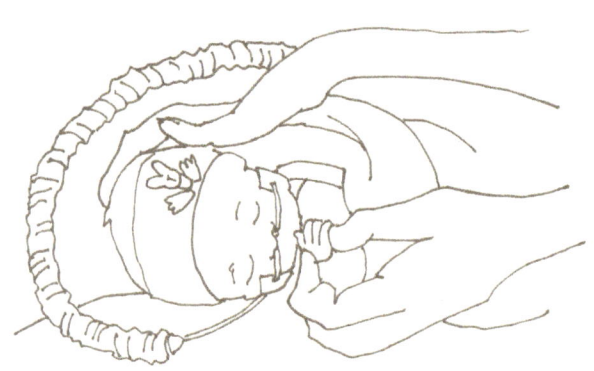

Grasping your finger, tucking into your hands, I feel supported and reassured.

Looking at your soft smile,
I am learning more each day.

Sucking for comfort and food,
I feel so calm in your embrace.

Sleeping peacefully in your arms,
I feel warm and relaxed with you.

Nestling on your chest,
I feel peaceful and cherished.

In each small, nurturing moment,
I grow bigger and stronger with you.

I am here...
and I know that you are too.
Being with you is everything.

You are your baby's
primary caregiver.

Watch and listen closely.
Your baby has many ways
of letting you know
their likes and needs
and desires.

Your earliest interactions with
your baby are both precious and important.
As you understand and respond
to your baby's unique ways
of communicating,
your loving relationship will grow.

Welcome, Little One

Name

Date of Birth

Age at Birth

Birthweight   Birth Length

Our Family, Our Story

This book about relationships is the product
of Deborah and Annie's treasured friendship
of over 40 years.

Deborah began her career as NIDCAP Founder Dr. Heidelise Als' first research assistant and became her collaborator in the development of NIDCAP. Deborah has a doctorate in developmental psychology and is dedicated to supporting the practice and training of NIDCAP and its global community.

Annie is an illustrator and graphic artist. She has taught drawing and book design for over 30 years. Annie's award-winning work is in collections in the United States, Hungary, Poland, Japan, and Turkey.

BEING WITH YOU IS EVERYTHING was inspired by the Newborn Individualized Developmental Care and Assessment Program (NIDCAP). This evidence-based caregiving approach was founded by Heidelise Als, PhD in the early 1980s.

NIDCAP helps premature and at-risk infants be understood and to have a voice in shaping their experiences within the hospital and beyond. NIDCAP appreciates that each infant's care and their development are most importantly nurtured by their own parents and families. Through healthy family relationships, experiences are optimized, and futures are improved.

NIDCAP care is becoming increasingly realized in hospitals all around the world. Please learn more about NIDCAP at www.nidcap.org.